blood desert

Mary Burritt
Christiansen
Poetry Series

Part of the
Mary Burritt Christiansen
Poetry Series

V. B. Price, *Series Editor*

**Also available in the University of New Mexico Press
Mary Burritt Christiansen Poetry Series:**

Poets of the Non-Existent City: Los Angeles in the McCarthy Era
edited by Estelle Gershgoren Novak

Selected Poems of Gabriela Mistral edited by Ursula K. Le Guin

Deeply Dug In by R. L. Barth

Amulet Songs: Poems Selected and New by Lucile Adler

In Company: An Anthology of New Mexico Poets After 1960
edited by Lee Bartlett, V. B. Price, and Dianne Edenfield Edwards

Tiempos Lejanos: Poetic Images from the Past by Nasario García

Refuge of Whirling Light by Mary Beath

The River Is Wide/El río es ancho: Twenty Mexican Poets, a Bilingual Anthology
edited and translated by Marlon L. Fick

A Scar Upon Our Voice by Robin Coffee

CrashBoomLove: A Novel in Verse by Juan Felipe Herrera

In a Dybbuk's Raincoat: Collected Poems by Bert Meyers

Rebirth of Wonder: Poems of the Common Life by David M. Johnson

Broken and Reset: Selected Poems, 1966 to 2006 by V. B. Price

The Curvature of the Earth by Gene Frumkin and Alvaro Cardona-Hine

Derivative of the Moving Image by Jennifer Bartlett

Map of the Lost by Miriam Sagan

¿de Veras?: Young Voices from the National Hispanic Cultural Center
edited by Mikaela Jae Renz and Shelle VanEtten-Luaces

A Bigger Boat: The Unlikely Success of the Albuquerque Poetry Slam Scene
edited by Susan McAllister, Don McIver, Mikaela Renz, and Daniel S. Solis

A Poetry of Remembrance: New and Rejected Works by Levi Romero

The Welcome Table by Jay Udall

How Shadows Are Bundled by Anne Valley-Fox

Bolitas de Oro by Nasario García

Astonishing Light by E. A. Mares

blood desert

WITNESSES
1820–1880

RENNY GOLDEN

UNIVERSITY OF NEW MEXICO PRESS

14   13   12   11   10   1   2   3   4   5

Library of Congress Cataloging-in-Publication Data

Golden, Renny.
Blood Desert : witnesses, 1820–1880 / Renny Golden.
p. cm.
ISBN 978-0-8263-4961-3 (pbk. : alk. paper)
1. New Mexico—Poetry.
I. Title.
PS3557.O35935B56 2010
811'.54—dc22
2010014704

Thanks to Katie Burke of Pomegrante Publishing for use of Meinrad's painting
published in *Meinrad Craighead: Crow Mother and Dog God, A Retropective*,
(Petaluma, CA: Pomegrante Communications), 2003, p. 107

The whole is lost / & we are fragments of those wagons moving west.

—Diane Glancy, *One Age in a Dream* (Milkweed, 1986)

Poetries are no more pure and simple than human histories are pure and simple. And there are colonized poetics and resilient poetics, transmissions across frontiers not easily traced.

—Adrienne Rich, *The Guardian*, Nov. 18, 2006

Contents

Timeline

1821   New Mexico becomes part of the new nation of Mexico, which has won its independence from Spain after three centuries of colonial rule.

1822   Antonio José Martínez is ordained a priest, after having lost his wife, María, during childbirth in 1813.

1842   Texans invade New Mexico, claiming that half the region (to the Rio Grande) belongs to the Republic of Texas; they are defeated.

1846   Brigadier General Stephen Watts Kearney and his Army of the West occupy New Mexico in the Mexican-American War.

1848   The Mexican-American War ends with the signing of the Treaty of Guadalupe-Hidalgo, which cedes half of Mexico, including New Mexico, to the United States.

1849   Gold Rush brings miners to the Southwest.

1850   Joined with Arizona, New Mexico (including what is now Arizona) becomes a territory of the United States.

1850   Quanah Parker, who will be chief of the Comanches, is born to his mother, Cynthia Ann Parker, and his father, Chief Peta Nocona.

1850   Rosa Maria Segale, who will become Sister Blandina, friend of outlaws, Utes, Navajos, and poor Mexicans in New Mexico, is born in Italy.

1851   Jean-Baptiste Lamy arrives in Santa Fe, becoming New Mexico's first Bishop.

1851   Four hundred Mexican soldiers attack an Apache camp, murdering
Geronimo's mother, wife, and three children in northern Mexico,
now a part of New Mexico; Geronimo spends the next thirty-five
years seeking revenge.

1852   Five Sisters of Loretto, a Catholic teaching order, arrive in Santa Fe
to open Loretto Academy, the first school for girls in New Mexico.

1857   Lozen, Apache shaman and sister of Chief Victorio, receives the
gift of prophecy in her ceremonial induction.

1858   Bishop Lamy excommunicates Padre Martínez in the culmination
of a prolonged clash between the French Lamy and native
Mexican priests.

1861   Apache Chief Cochise, falsely accused of kidnapping, is arrested
and then escapes.

1862   At Apache Pass, Cochise and five hundred warriors hold off
U.S. Army troops firing howitzers.

1865   Nurse Catherine Mallon, with three other Sisters of Charity,
opens the first makeshift hospital in Santa Fe.

1867   Treaty of Medicine Lodge confines the Plains Indians to a
reservation. Quanah Parker, Comanche Chief, refuses, fights
against Colonel Mackenzie, is never captured.

1870   General Crook, the great Indian fighter, is ordered to arrest
Standing Bear, Chief of the Poncas, because he left a forced
march in a Plains winter to return to Ponca land in order to
bury his son who died of pneumonia.

1871   General Crook uses Apache scouts to track Cochise.

1872   Sister of Charity Blandina builds the first school in Trinidad,
Colorado; later builds schools in New Mexico.

1876   U.S. Army sends 5,000 soldiers and 500 Apache scouts to track
and capture the elusive Geronimo.

1877   Another Apache Chief, Victorio, is ordered to San Carlos
reservation but the conditions are so deplorable that he escapes
to Mexico.

1880   Chief Victorio is surrounded, killed in Mexico. Thereafter, Lozen
rides with Apache leaders Geronimo and Nana.

1886   At Lozen's urging, Geronimo surrenders to General Crook, but he
later escapes.

1886   Geronimo surrenders to General Miles, who promises the band
can remain in their territory.

1886   General Miles instead sends the Apaches to a Florida swamp area.

Foreword

As a sociologist, theology professor, and tireless activist, Renny Golden has spent her life helping those in need, from former prisoners looking for work and immigrants seeking sanctuary from war zones in Central America to maximum security inmates wanting an education and imprisoned mothers and their desperate families.

In *Blood Desert*, poet Renny Golden brings to life a violent era in New Mexican history, filled with the courage of nuns and nurses who brought education and succor to a world torn by the American war with Mexico, the U.S. Civil War, religious struggles between Bishop Lamy and Padre Martínez, the Long March of the Navajos, and the ambushes and betrayals of the last days of the Apache Wars.

In a rich combination of fictional first-person monologues and third person poetic epic narratives, Golden gives voice to the great spirits of the age—many of them women whose devotion and heroism are often overshadowed in the historical record. Her empathetic inward seeing into their lives and struggles is sharpened by her own experience in war-torn, harsh, and violent environments. When Golden writes that "The nuns have left small footprints in / a desert that expects no allies," there's an authenticity that cuts to the bone. The reader feels Golden understands these intrepid souls, and the land that tempered them, from the inside out.

The Loretto and Charity sisters accompany
the wretched as if they held Mystery
in torn, filthy breast pockets. What do they cling

to as their time ends, the hour of nuns
archaic as cowboys?

In a poem called "Priests of the Plains, 1850," she pairs two births
that year, one of a Comanche and the other of an Italian—Quanah Parker,
the half-breed Comanche leader who was never defeated, and Rosa Maria
Segale, called Sister Blandina, a champion of children, a devoted teacher
who dedicated her life to education in New Mexico and Southern Colorado,
and an acquaintance of Billy the Kid.

Sister Blandina "pulls // her valise from the train, its small contents
/meek, her inner baggage, huge, holy, / theatrical, a spirit that matches
cowboy / Colorado's call for the rugged and the lost."

Golden's human understanding has the generosity that comes from
having gone into her own depths to find responses to the painful and trou-
bling situations of the past she explores. When she writes about Geronimo
in captivity, the reader feels as if Golden was speaking through his life.

I want to break your
trust the way Mexicans broke my wife, my mother,
my three babies, their scalps in blood rivers. What
fear can you offer a dead man? After that

I did not pray . . . I had no purpose left. I could not
call back my loved ones. I could not bring back
dead Apaches but I could rejoice in . . . revenge.

. . . I am not trustworthy. I am wily,
a coyote slipping into shadow. . . .

What did you expect . . . truth? Whose?

The values and world view in Renny Golden's poems here are consistent with
her other writings, among them: *Lost Voices: a Multicultural History of the
United States 1500s–1860, Oscar Romero: Reflections on His Life and Writings,
The Hour of the Furnaces* (a book of poems and prose on the social history
of the war years in Central America), and *War on the Family: Imprisoned
Mothers and the Families They Leave Behind.* Poetic narratives written in an
epic voice interspersed with imaginative autobiographical monologues of

major historic characters are rarities in contemporary American poetry. *Blood Desert* focuses the political and moral intensity of Renny Golden's life and philosophy through the emotional clarity of her poetic practice. These poems treat one of New Mexico's most turbulent eras with a sense of justice and compassion that dramatically brings to life the human grandeur of New Mexico history.

—V. B. Price, Albuquerque

Introduction

I sought New Mexico for old reasons . . . the silence and mystery of the high desert, perhaps the last of America's wild country. The Sandia and Sangre de Cristo mountains hunch beneath a turquoise sky swimming with Moby Dick whale clouds in a vast, stunning silence and a presence that I can only describe as holy. Santa Clara Pueblo Indian Rina Swentzell links breath with the spirit of the peoples of the land: *What we are told as children is that people when they walk on the land leave their breath wherever they go. So wherever we walk, that particular spot on the earth never forgets us, and when we go back to these places, we know that the people who have lived there are in some way still there, and that we can actually partake of their breath and their spirit.*

I could not know whose bones I walked across but I knew the land held the frail breath of those who belonged to the land, loved it, and died defending it. New Mexico invites interrogation. Not simply the mystery of what happened to the ancient Anasazi peoples but the more recent history of the "founding" of New Mexico in the 1800s. Historians have called U.S. General Kearney's 1846 march of 3,000 soldiers into Santa Fe a peaceful takeover. But I'd read poets Simon Ortiz and Tony Mares, as well as historians Roxanne Dunbar Ortiz and Rodolfo Acuña, and I knew the terror that preceded (and followed) that occupation.

Those whose spirits breathe the arroyos, canyons, and mesas—Pueblo, Apache, Navajo, Zuni, Hopi, Mexican farmers—were not the only peoples of the land, which is also inhabited by the spirits of those who came: the conquerors, the adventurers, the impoverished, the dreamers, the outlaws, Americans who traveled the Santa Fe Trail seeking fortune or a chance.

Some came for neither. Male ecclesiastics came for souls. In her novel *Death Comes for the Archbishop*, Willa Cather valorized the leader of the New Mexican church, Bishop Jean-Baptiste Lamy. But Lamy was not the architect of New Mexico's church. A Mexican church already existed, led by Padre Antonio José Martínez, Lamy's nemesis. Additionally, no one noticed the church's actual "builders," a group of women almost as historically invisible as native women—the Sisters of Loretto and the Sisters of Charity who rode the Trail to the frontier in order to build schools and hospitals, to nurse renegades, peasants, and the destitute.

I read the diary of feisty Sister Blandina, the speeches of Geronimo, the regret of General Crook for his treatment of indigenous peoples in New Mexico and Nebraska, the excommunication of Padre Martínez, of Kit Carson's siege of Canyon de Chelly and the Navajo Long March, and I wanted their voices to be heard again. Their breath is here where the wind-rocked sandstone canyons and solitary piñon-studded woods hold a sacred bloodstained history. These narrative poems intend to reclaim dangerous memory, to resurrect the spirit of those who walked and rode the high desert thick with blooms of globe mallow, white chicory, wooly daisies and sudden carpets of purple verbena spread out in the sand. Why poetry and not history? Poetry seems to match the music and mystery of a time of betrayal and bravery. Poetry can be an act of accompaniment that imitates the native way that Apache Phillip Cassadore describes: *We say, "I walk with you," not "I walk before you" or "I walk behind you." . . . You are not a leader, you are a part.*

Renny Golden

Story In Bone, Sand, Rock

Nuevo México

The high desert is a dog with no sense
of time. Its two-legged family might have left
yesterday or five hundred years ago.

The dog wags its tail, the desert blooms.
On the sweeps of pine-scented mountains,
in parched beds, orange mesas,

stippled canals where ducks drift
a mud-brown Rio Grande, the land remembers,
buries its story in stone, sand, and bones.

Los Ladrones (The Thieves)

I. Taos, Mexico, 1813

Antonio José's knees buckle when the Thief enters.
He cradles his baby anointed in her mother's dying sweat,
smells his wife, María, in the whimpering bundle,
knows he will forget the scent, knows the flame

of his heart flickers lower and lower. He does not yet know
the tiny thief in his arms, how she will steal him.
The next death is all he wants. He names the baby
María de la Luz. In her dark eyes he sees blazing canyons,

pale arroyos, casks of yellow columbine, extravagance
everywhere. All he did not see, whispers, intimate as a father
listening to a child's soft breathing in the dark. Was it death,
that *vaquero*, racing a stallion past Antonio José only to halt

up ahead? Horse and rider, silhouettes. Was it loneliness
of the forsaken, the family of the crushed to whom he belonged?
Was it holy ghosts, the Holy Ghost? What Antonio José Martínez
wants is to rise selfless, a priest who dies slow and joyful

in the service of *los pobres*. He leaves for Mexico's Seminary.
What he leaves will not leave him. *Papi, Papi*
is all he hears in a desert mute with starlight. *Papi, Papi*
in canyons, his four year old crying in Abuela's arms. He wants

to turn back. This is Antonio José's first death. He keeps riding.
When the ordination Bishop calls his name, María's father,
lying prostrate before the altar, rises, answers: *Adsum, I am here.*
I am here by virtue of love. She who breathes in me, María, adsum.

This love is what you called forth. His seven year old sits
in a cathedral pew snuffed by shadow watching *Papi* walk
toward a gold leaf altar, his white linen alb dazzling. She does not wave
when *Papi* turns, a smudge of holy oil glistening on his forehead.

II. Tomé, México

Padre Antonio José preaches to ragged farmers in a rural chapel
hunched below mesas of howling wolves. Antonio José, too, sings:
sly as a coyote, even the men return to Mass. The people
are scripture. María, his joy, takes his arm, walks a trail

of dogwood, Spanish broom, purple laurel. Wind bounces
tumbleweed against a cracked adobe church where Antonio José
pours water on the foreheads of raven-haired children, sprinkles
coffins of *los ancianos*, blesses young lovers whose vows

bring him to tears. His twelve year old is dying. Antonio José's
prayers are a snow drift piled against the doors of heaven.
María de la Luz enters light that waited in every breath,
her black eyes asking him to explain. The people are the sea

where he drowns. He rides his mare to each priestless church
in Abiquiu. He genuflects before naked olive trees
knuckling out winter. He carries candles, wafers, linen
altar cloth, a bottle of wine because the people are too poor.

Their gratitude floods the house of death he carries. Antonio
accepts their tithes of honey and cornmeal. Who knows
their hunger for beans, a few tortillas, chicken on holidays?
The other hunger, to believe in *La Virgen*, in all they cannot

see, that world of spirits, of a Holy Spirit that favors the poor.
To feed this hunger, they give away produce, steal *fanegas* of corn
to pay for a wedding, a baptism. Antonio José writes Mexico:
Our people are hungry for God, hungry for bread, too.

Sacraments here are for the rich. Abolish tithes!
Padre Antonio wants a church of, *not for*, the poor. Bishop Lamy
wants French cathedrals. Rome wants tithes. Americans want
to own the shadows and each valley's bowl of light. *Gringos*

want Pueblo hunting grounds, Apache's sacred mountains, want
each grain of sand. Martínez drafts paper weapons, crumpled
in the hands of officials. Ignored, he publishes a treatise. It quivers,
a perfectly thrown knife, wedged deep in Bishop Lamy's cathedral door.

Padre Antonio José Martínez

We taught our arms to whip our
shoulders to an ooze of blood stars.
The plum-blue wounds were our choice.

We, *los penitentes,* took *el salvador's*
pain . . . brilliant, brave, macabre.
Franciscans sang it to our cradles,

its dark pageantry and crown of thorns
thrilled our childhoods, Our holiness
was to be ignored by Mexico, Spain, Rome,

by new occupiers giddy with war.
Bluecoats, Greycoats marched through us
as if we were ghosts because we were,

orphans who invented ourselves, *mestizaje,*
invisible as the holy spirit whom no bishop
could recognize. We are cliff rose, Apache plume

after desert rains, manzanita buds in the mountain's toes.
We are the desert's hungry people; a river brings us
canticles of sandhill cranes, lamentations of geese. Do

you know what these farmers gave us ?
All they had. Respect, well, that was for Bishops.
We were *bandidos, borrachos,* mountains kept us safe,

happy among the dead with their dancing mud boots
tracked into adobe chapels, the rafters hung with bats,
spider silk. We, who ate lizards, had no grand narratives,

no cassocks stained with French wine,
nothing was ours except the Rio Grande
which the gringos took anyway.

We were not even interesting sinners. We were
the recipients of grace, never the bearers.
Franciscans took holiness when they left, packing it

like tamales for a long trip. Blessing eluded us
until we fought back. Than we became reprobates
that Bishop Lamy and Vicar Macheboeuf

disowned—as if we ever belonged to
those we taught to ride, to speak to spirits,
animals, yucca, our God of the abandoned

who took my vows, never complained, never
asked for tithes, cathedrals, property or
submission, never abandoned us.

Bishop Lamy

I. Auvergne, France

I was born among cherry orchards,
starlings fluttered amidst a twilight
of bells. When I dream, I am

a boy in our village listening to
a Voice that waited in time,
marking the hours, faithful

as François, the sacristan whose gnarled
hands pulled bell ropes. My fidelity, too,
was generous but not, alas, hidden. My chum

Joseph Macheboeuf saw to it that we would
not remain unknown country priests, or was
it my own ambition, not for fame, but fierce

loyalty to the Church, God's vessel? More timid,
I was a wolfhound lopping behind Macheboeuf,
a scrappy terrier who would bite too quickly.

Did I remember this when our ideals were coins
we could not spend? I wanted useful hands, a priest's,
to release magic, doves of blessing ascending

from the Hidden. I still see the cathedral's windows
filling ruby gold, as we moved, like thieves, through
dawn-brushed streets bound for America's missions.

II. 1851, The Frontier

How could we have known how desert
light tricks the eye, canyons drinking wine skies,
lavender bellflowers sputtered on the sand floor?

I never lusted for crosier and staff, episcopal
purple and lace. Did I lose this innocence, or did
duty, harsh and merciful, demand armor I could

no more abandon than forsake French propriety?
What more forbearance for renegade Mexican
priests could I give? Yes, I excommunicated them

one after another, drunkards, womanizers, gamblers.
Yes, I forbid the *fandango*, its invitation to
licentiousness. The New Mexican wound was

deep, so I bled the patient to save it. Yes, I rode
thousands of sand trails, lips blistered, eyes crusted,
lifted broken wagon axles, coaxed mule teams

across rutted prairies, all to guide Sisters through
Comanche territory, to bring French priests
overland. Yes, I rebuilt a church of stooped mud

stables to glory-houses of leaded glass, fluted columns,
pilasters. Heaven's symbol in a barren place. Schools, too,
for Mexican and Indian children, a hospital with gods

who pitted their magic against typhoid and hepatitis.
Yes, I forbade *santero* art, statues with grotesque
wooden eyes. Yes, I ordered tithes or denial of sacraments.

Vicar Macheboeuf railed *damnation* or *submission*. Yes, they petitioned
Rome against us. Too late. Macheboeuf wrote first of New Mexicans
little accustomed to governing themselves . . . ignorant men, corrupt,

their prejudice toward a foreign bishop obliged reform of their morals.
Yes, our priests failed too, but four, only four scandalized. I moved
them without hesitation. Yes, I sent Macheboeuf to excommunicate

Antonio José Martínez. I had no recourse. I was a shepherd amongst
starving sheep. Regrets? Martínez was their Bishop as much as I.
If he refused tithes, the house would fall. We were both zealots.

Antonio's nature, unlike Macheboeuf's, was calm as mine, as
sure. Yes, Bishop Macheboeuf never kept an opinion to himself.
He called suffragettes *short-haired women and long-haired men,*

then suspended Sister Fidelis when she challenged him.
Yet Macheboeuf, my guard dog, blamed me for Antonio José.
His regret? My terrier left Martínez damned, then complained:

It is always the way. Bishop Lamy is sure to send me when a bad
case is to be settled; I am always the one to whip the cats.
Yes, I brought artisans from the Old World, and, yes, I wore

that world's damask-threaded vestments, white moiré stole
embroidered with red crosses and jewels . . . trappings for others.
Daily I wore sweat-ringed breeches on desert trails. To baptize,

I rode from Albuquerque to San Francisco praying with the Zuni
who called me *Tata*. I slept on saddlebags, one eye open
in Apache country. I rode Granite Mountain's cedar forests filling

with thick snow muffling hoofbeats. My fingers swollen that
morning when I said Mass for twenty-five good souls kneeling
on wood planks and evergreen boughs for La Navidad. In the Mojave

I understood the sacrament of water, prayed for Apache stamina.
We rode the silver desert for six months, a thousand sacraments.
I was fifty years old, never stumbled until Mesilla two days

from home. Weakness, that thief, knocked me from my horse.
I fought it, gripped a saddle horn, remounted, crossed
the Rio Grande at 3 a.m., hungry, not for food, I starved

for home, Santa Fe. Yes, I rode again and again, once,
behind General Carleton, pitied Apaches and Navajos
he penned like cattle at Bosque Redondo. Yes, our Pueblo

and Navajo schools failed from lack of government funds not
mercy. If I have failed it is not *seven miserable priests*,
especially Vicar Juan Felipe Ortiz, or Padre Gallegos

who denounced me in the *Gazette*, tattled to Rome. No, my regret
is that I, *Tata*, had nothing to pay teachers for Pueblos.
My accounts: 135 churches; 9 schools; a hospital; a seminary.

III. 1888, Villa Pintoresca Ranchito

Sometimes now I forget French. Auvergne fades,
though the Voice that first whispered calls from
Tesuque hills and Jemez mountains as if nothing

came before this light anointing my peach orchards,
strawberry fields, and, yes, cherry orchards.
This October procession—with its scent of smoking piñon

and bobbing flames to honor St. Francis' wily loves—
is my last. As if I too were a beggar burning my last candle:
You burning sun, you silver moon. Alleluia!

Priests of the Plains, 1850

Anoint these infants, oil them for a spirit journey.
These two who will remember the star burned
across their tiny hearts: a Comanche, an Italian.
These two who took nothing except desert chicory,

purple sage because the flowers rose from sand,
because what you cherish offers itself, creosote and
butcher's bloom, jackrabbit and moon.
It is 1850, northern Mexico has been lassoed.

> *The babies smile and nuzzle mothers who*
> *don't want prophets but cannot help themselves.*
> *Magdalenes, spendthrifts, who whisper: the people.*
> *Oh you who baptize in milk and honey, women*
> *who slip into history invisible as spiders*
> *pulling silk across the heavens nothing can break.*

Two babies bawl into America's holy rooms.
Others will name them, twice. Quanah Parker
and Rosa Maria Segale receive spirit names:
Nermernuh Tseeta and Sister Blandina.

Twenty years later, black-robed Blandina
rides the Trail, her bonnet tied with a black bow,
her almond eyes amused and intense at
the same time. Sister Blandina pulls

her valise from the train, its small contents
meek, her inner baggage, huge, holy,
theatrical, a spirit that matches cowboy
Colorado's call for the rugged and the lost.

Twenty years from birth, comes Quanah Parker,
Comanche Chief, buckskin leggings grip stallion's
ribs, beaver oil on his chest, a warbonnet of eagle
feathers opens in wind's hands, pulls back his black

braid woven of otter fur, red flannel ribbon. The pale
eyes of a mixed-blood measures the enemy: his mother's
people, who will never capture him, who carry doom
through seasons of moon and cranes.

Las Hermanas de la Luz (Sisters of the Light)

I. Kentucky Motherhouse Chapel, 1852

The Sisters of Loretto genuflect, kiss silver crosses,
ready for the journey to Santa Fe, land
Indians call Dancing Ground of the Sun.
Rose flakes of light fall on oak pews where Sisters

intone Te Deum. A gauze of incense floats up,
disappears. Six missionaries stand amidst candles
that flicker like heartbeats. The Congregation raises hands
held steady as hummingbirds, the flock of hands anoint

six bowed heads. Benediction falls like an ax.
As a sickle fells a wheat field, so vows cut.
Promises that invite the hunger road, its luminous
trail opening stones, canyons, hearts. The choir sings

Canticle of the Sun while a processional of black robes
winds outside into sycamore shade blackening
moss gardens, Motherhouse lawns. Then it begins:
journey to Santa Fe that only four of the six will live to see.

> *What do you bring to protect yourself when the glory
> road rises, running with rivers, open skies, lavender hills,
> a desert of orphans, sick miners, bandits . . .
> a road map soaked in blood? Do you go suspicious,
> a cynic's heart your shield, or the sister's road, dauntless,
> naive, bringing mule-thick service and no regrets?*

II. Mississippi River

Mother Matilda leans on the rail of the Kansas steamer,
looks toward Missouri where fear, an apocalyptic horse,
pulls back, paws, its hooves pound delirious.
How will they cross desert, mountains, Indian territory

on a trail made by mavericks and staked with white crosses
for those who fell to typhoid or dysentery?
*Will my sisters, dragging full-length serge habits through mud
and tumbleweed, pass like dark angels through the mountains?*

God willing, she prays, opening her palms in surrender.
On the green river banks poplars shimmer dusky gold.
That night Mother Matilda cannot catch her breath. Cholera.
Night-watch of steamed towels, elderberry bark syrup. *Breathe,*

breathe, please Mother. On the nineteenth day out,
passengers hear the Sisters sing *In Paradisum.*
The diminished choir intones: *May the angels lead you into paradise.*
Matilda will never see a low ridge of white buffalo clouds,

never see Our Lady of Light chapel rise
like a house of dawn. Did Matilda hear the intonation
begin, the small, choked sopranos? Did she hear a last prayer
lift up, a bit flat, but confident? Did she smile?

III. Blue Hills Landing

The QUARANTINE sign floats its order on an aqua pasture.
Sisters Magdalen Hayden and Monica Bailey stare glassy-eyed,
faces milky, feverish. Sister Catherine's hands tremble pitching
tents; cots that float them like ghost boats into frenzied dreams where

Magdalen watches the moon throw its silver cape on a hissing prairie,
her cracked lips parting for breath. She winces with each squeeze
of rib cage but does not yelp, faithful as her dog bringing sheep
until her beloved Collie ran the woolies a last time, slumped,

obedient unto death. Delirious, Magdalen sees a white owl,
hears it call her name in Spanish: *Magdalena, venga.*
Come where: heaven or the Dancing Ground of the Sun?
Sister Monica moans. Dangerously weak, she must turn back.

On the Mississippi, Monica watches a hawk soar
then twist back as if the bird could ride any current home.
Monica, too, promises to twist back west. God willing,
she vows. The hawk drops off a cloud, disappears.

Would you fight the thief pulling you toward sleep,
no, toward oblivion, in order to board a stagecoach
that rattles the bones of your eye sockets headed
into sacred lands of starving Comanches?
Would the summons of the land of sun
and stone make you fierce or weak?

Magdalen Hayden carries her bag to the stagecoach,
refuses help from the vicar apostolic of New Mexico.
The vicar's collar, a white moth, bobs with his Adam's apple,
flutters above his trail-coat, muddied boots.

Bones aching, woozy, Magdalen bumps, sways,
watches clouds darken tall grass until black rain
punches horses. Wind tears tents from their hands.
The nuns huddle in a wind-slammed coach. Outside

the prairie cracks open in silver explosions.
Magdalen tells her diary: *terrific storm*
made (our) frail tenement sway to and fro
creak as if ready to fall to pieces.

At Pawnee Creek, stillness lifts prayers of coyotes, owls,
Indians, the Sisters. Magdalen dreams ruby rivers,
buffalo in Comanche masks sing *In Paradisum.* Snow-white
owls speak in Spanish again: ¡ven ahora! come now!

Outside Fort Atkinson, gripped knuckles turn to white marble.
Four hundred Indians ride out of the whip of dust.
Hooves drum alongside wagons that violate sacred ground.
On command, the wall of red hunters fades back into

curtains of dust lifting. The travelers thank God, not the Kiowa.
To cross Kansas, drivers whisper in the ears of exhausted horses
to pull, pull through a moonless night. By day, buffalo hammer
the plains, hoof marks flaking like dried blood. Comanches enter

the music of canyons where shadows praise, winds clap hands,
warblers, coyote sing. Natives will never join the *civilized* orchestra
even now crossing the prairies with harpsichords, bassoons, cellos;
will not build chapels of mortar, stained glass filtering sunlight.

IV. Santa Fe Mission, Where the Trail Ends

Outside Santa Fe, the Sisters slap at black habits, butterflies
of trail dust rise into dry blue air. As their wagon train
approaches, shouts go up: *Las Madres, Las Madres,*
which ignites music. Alberto Gonzales stomps

three times and *guitarras* play a *ranchero*. José,
the sacristan, yanks the rope bells as if it were Easter.
The children stand beneath silk banners embroidered
by grandmothers who have waited for the teachers for two

generations of Mexicans. *Comadres* pass out *maiz* tortillas thick
with frijoles and onions which they offer beggars, like priests
giving communion. In their midst, Bishop Lamy leads
a procession of boys in cassocks swinging tin crucibles of burning

incense, advancing with gold crosses bobbing in the smoked air.
Burros, dogs trot across narrow streets as if they, too, might sing.
Bishop Lamy squints into light washing four black figures,
spirit walkers who take the soul road; a confederacy

who cross mountains to match magic with *curanderas*,
shamans, medicine women; flamers who will run
like a prairie fire. Lamy sighs, at last, bodies free
as a Paschal candle to burn until they flicker out. The nuns

hesitate, stand beneath a wall blazing with bougainvillea. Catherine
Mahoney, Rosanna Dant, and Roberta Brown wait for Magdalen
to greet the Bishop first. *Mother Magdalen*, the sisters say,
when the people meet them. Farmers, children, grasp their hands:

benedicamus. Magdalen knows so little Spanish. She nods,
bows, *Gracias, gracias.* The people's words fly from their mouths,
small birds she can't catch. Magdalen feels tongueless, her words
tied to a stake. She knows such loss, her own native Irish, forbidden,

her mother whispered the old language, a ghost in the house. Magdalen
wants a eucharist of language so that she can be broken open.
Her teachers, two Mexican sisters, are the young priests who place
the bread of language on her tongue.

I am Margarita, seventeen years old. Las Hermanas say amor
but they only mean God, not our mountains, roses, cornfields,
not hombres, like Felipe, his eyes black rivers, lips soft as mangos,
no, never amor like that. Francisquita grows more like them each day,
her eyes, dark coins she spends in chapel before La Virgen,
the gold box of God. I teach them language, she teaches trust.

V. Academy of Our Lady of Light

The sisters rise before dawn star, stand in a mud chapel
singing *Ave Maris Stella*, their sopranos lifting in apricot light.
In the garden, sweat opens dark flowers in the armpits
of Sister Catherine's habit. She hoes bean rows, tomatoes,

carrots. Sister Rosanna bags produce, drags sacks to a market wagon
that smells of moist soil, leaked melon juice, onions, *limón*.
The garden will pay for the first frontier school that will not
be for future soldiers, cowboys, statesman . . . but for girls. An academy

of Our Lady of Light named for a Maria of desert and stone
who took no offense at miracles, spoke with angels,
bore a son who kissed lepers, called landless peasants to believe
heaven rested, small as a mustard seed, in earth's bruised body.

Magdalen walks beside Francisquita who touches
scarlet flax, prairie zinnia, repeats their Spanish names.
Spanish is wine Magdalen drinks wildly, injudiciously.
She loves to say: alabanza, praise.
Alabanza for the Mexican people who say
"May God go with you" instead of good-bye.

The Sisters teach languages, too. *I find the girls docile*, writes
Magdalen, but *they have a strong predilection for music.* What violins
play beneath the girl's decorum, what oboe weeps inside?
The girls have more talent for imitation than for the sciences.

Spunky Marian Russell never learned the sciences, etiquette,
or Catholicism. The nuns called her *our little heretic.*
What she learned, she taught herself: to gallop her pinto,
a dog who flew to her whistle, herbs for snakebites. But one

lesson took: *Every day we were supposed to do something for others.*
Little heretic endured Latin hymns, wood kneelers for the rosary,
never became a Catholic, never became a lady,
never forgot to feed the hungry and clothe the naked.

VI. The Mud Roof Convent

Rains fall through red bud trees, drum the chicken coop,
pour off milking stalls into puddles ringing the garden.
The clotted roof drips rain in every room, streaking
walls with chocolate grit, opening puddles of mud

pancakes. To spare his gold-threaded vestments, hand-stitched
by elderly French nuns, Bishop Lamy stands in the pulpit
with an umbrella in his hand; he eats oysters in the refectory
holding the umbrella over a table of tortillas while next door

the Sisters of Loretto play chess with the adobe's brown rains:
We have been moving our beds from place to place
in order to find a dry spot. White linen, altar cloth
soiled with brown rings, slivers of light leak through cracks in

the tiny chapel walls where sputtering candles
throw light against stained, musty walls. The nuns walk
on dreaming feet, their boots caked. Tiny silver bugs swim
in the basins and cisterns. When smallpox breaks out, ominous

as a mad clown painting faces with bright pockmarks, the Sisters
check the girls nightly, slip through the dormitories smiling,
reassuring, observant as botanists among threatened flowers.
The nuns boil vats of water that send up plumes of steam

crumpling Sister Catherine's bonnet. Magdalen enters the infirmary
fearless, inoculated by cholera, La Virgen, and the white owl.
The sisters scald everything, scrub wood to the color of clouds.
Even when typhoid slips in, the nuns win each girl's recovery.

> *They walk on tiptoe through wards of death*
> *frogs and flowers swimming in the garden, owls*
> *and mice hidden, waiting for the moon, patient*
> *as girls who learn to pray in Latin. Deo gratias when*
> *the skies open indigo clear, silver moons pour through*
> *apple orchards, cover the sheds with alabaster light.*

VII. Civil War Comes to Santa Fe

For miles you can see Texas Mounted Volunteers advancing, purple
dust mushrooming in crystal air. In the Plaza, horses, slick with foam,
circle, whinny, clop to a standstill. The animals are spent from weeks
in the Sonora trotting past cholla, horsebrush, giant saguaro with its

nesting holes of elf owls whoo-whooing. The Texan Confederates, under General Sibley, "take" Santa Fe as if it were a wild horse any cowboy could break. Santa Fe's ragged Bluecoat army has left for Fort Union, left the city defenseless, silent. Before the Unionists

rode out, the Sisters called them *our boys* but watched as they became arsonists, burned down barracks, houses, sacks of flour as they pulled out. The flame-whooshing haystacks in the army's corral burned open a hole in the night that the nuns recognize.

> *Always women standing in the charred house,*
> *a stink of death on their clothes, gathering children*
> *who will remember father calling from the grave*
> *venganza, venganza. Mothers offer bread,*
> *but warriors hold out stones of patria*
> *that children eat, turn their hearts to stone.*

VIII. Occupied Santa Fe

Academy is closed. Greycoats shout orders, wagons rumble, artillery wagons, past the walled convent garden. Santa Fe curls into a ball, positioning for the battering. Burros, dogs, inside. *Silencio!* Elena whispers when

little Luis strums *Papi's* guitar. Cannons alone have tongues, voices that puncture sound. Music is forbidden, except the defiant bells of Santa Fe. At Matins, Lauds, they ring across rooftops, over

the cienega, across arroyos, above the Santa Fe River stippled with shadows of wild geese. *I feared that our house would be burned or thrown down by the cannon balls,* Mother Magdalen writes in her diary while bells chime off-key.

> *The stubborn burro bells of Santa Fe ring for children*
> *who could not go to school, for terrified mothers, for an enemy*
> *who will ride south, a ravaged cavalry of ghosts. The bells,*
> *a pathetic orchestra, play their anthem like deaf musicians who*
> *will not leave the stage. The Confederates saddle up in the belling*
> *air, clappers pounding Ave Maria above their retreat.*

Steadfast as the bells, Magdalen re-opens the Academy. The ordinary glory of teaching, planting, baking, milking is miraculous as crocuses. For fifteen years Magdalen opens schools. New Sisters will ride the Chili Line, watch lavender plains, wild horses, dung mountains. No owls speak to them.

IX. The Legacy

Mother Magdalen walks the garden lush with apple blossoms, borders
of daffodils run the rock wall. Colors blur now, distant mountains
that whispered: *steadfast, steadfast,* have grown dim. The nun's dog
nudges her hand and she remembers her childhood sheepdog

racing over the clovered bog side of Rath-Clough Ireland, that cold,
jeweled land where she was a girl walking toward the cliffs facing
America, walking toward a chasm of promises she would make at nineteen,
a nun who would speak Spanish with a brogue, listen to owls,

design a Gothic chapel cut out of red earth set with jeweler's
precision at the end of the Santa Fe Trail. She remembers it all,
how Archbishop Jean-Baptiste Lamy, Obispo Juan, rode
3,000 trail miles on stallions and the bay mule he named,

El Bendito Frijole y El Santo Atole (blessed bean and holy cornmeal mush),
the stern dreamer who walked stiffly behind Mexicans slapping
tambourines, strumming guitars to accompany the dead well
beyond music's happy company. That same Frenchman

loved *el pueblo,* hated their flat roofs, desired a Romanesque
Cathedral, high arches, blue leaded windows, organ music lifting
toward frescoed angels, wanted European scale not squat,
mud-bleached, lightless churches. Patron, who called the Lorettos

over the plains so long ago, who loved French aesthetic, roof fleurs-de-lis,
gypsum moldings, who *told* Magdalen how the Chapel would rise, just as he
knuckled Padre Martínez who did not agree a Louis IX Sainte-Chapelle would
open heaven. *Gracias,* Magdalen said, but Lorettos pay for their own chapel.

You who today look up to twelve petaled crimson windows,
who touch sandstone pulleyed from Cerro Colorado quarry,
laid by thick-fingered Italian stonemasons who hunched with German
and Mexican carpenters beneath porch shade taking soup and tortillas
from Sister Rosanne's kitchen; you drawn to light streaming ruby,
blue-gold fish hand-blown by French artisans; you who marvel at the spiral
staircase that impossibly suspends in air; you astonished by the Chapel of Our
Lady of Light rising above the river, luminous in late afternoon, sculpted,
chiseled, and carved by the calloused, beautiful hands of immigrants—
pay heed to the other beauty, the people who taught Lamy to dance,
who gave the Lorettos a sun which outshone cathedrals, ochre stones
heavier than conquest, poverty like bread broken open and surprising.

Light comes down in gold flakes, the blazing world, filmy.
Magdalen's weary eyes unafraid as the fiery desert hills fall to shadow.
Memory throws up color, a white owl in a green pasture, velvet hills of Ireland,
a garden of tiger lilies, purple aster drunk with New Mexico's tawny light.

Venga, venga long after Magdalen's summons is silent.

Mother Magdalen Hayden

Even as a Kilkenny five year old
I knew how to do things, rise
with the last star to dress the babies,

pour milk in saucers, glints of light
pearling a grey dawn. Generosity,
a necessity for Irish peasants, was natural

as heather-gashed fields, our lush Rath-Clough
bogside stunned with sunlight
the surprise of it in our clotted sky.

When we left the farm I cried for
our collie but didn't tell Mother. What is
learned early is an instinct to be of use.

I didn't vow fidelity as much as I was
given it in those impaled potato fields.
I knew early, too, that geographies,

are betrayed by those who are tattered
as well as those who trample. Borders are dirt
and vows: to be kept, to be swept away. We

immigrants are beggars no tears comfort:
what quivers in memory, still as a hummingbird,
is a flash of land, sheep dog, all that hovers, sweeps

off. I am Irish. I am a Loretto. I am American.
I am New Mexican. I am old. I have never
refused the owl's call.

A Stone Along the Way

Manifest Destiny

These stones aren't sad.

—Pablo Neruda, in "To the Traveler"

While the names of God were spoken
we changed the stars, rearranged rivers
for their own sake. We made the desert safe
for music and owls. An army of destiny

stormed the plains, leather fists, promises
furled. This new land, of prophets and profiteers,
courage flung like coins we could spare.
Yankee Providence rode into the mountains,

lit campfires, bugled the tall grass
with audacity and small regret. America
of fluted plains never so sorry as history complains.
New Mexico was a stone on the way.

Canyon de Chelly, 1864

I was stone, will be stone
  —Joy Harjo, from "House"

I

Snow carpets a sandstone table rising one
thousand feet from the canyon floor. From there
Navajos watch specks below, Bluecoats, small
as toy soldiers, their miniature horses halt before

the canyon's mouth. Three hundred hollow-eyed
Navajo, Diné, have climbed sacred cliff rock, elders
pulled up, wisps of their silver hair, tiny wings. Cold stings
eyes, their hands like bruised apples where they grip

handholds cut by young men strapped with pouches
of berries, mutton, nuts. Muscled boys who rise like
angels to the house of sky, then run down hidden
stairs to carry up infants. Safe on Forest Rock, soaring

in clouds, great mother turtle carrying a nation on
her shell. The Diné walk on her frozen back reverent
as monks, chant to her, to the gods who wait there. Snow
floats over piñon, spruce. Colonel Kit Carson's dragoons

wait below, their horses paw muffs of feathered snow.
Carson edges forward, reins in. His uniform jacket
is powdered. Carson is not a West Pointer, cannot read
his written orders. Beaver, bears, wolves taught him

languages General Carleton will never understand.
Navajos taught him silence, how to read clouds. He will
not enter the canyon blurred white, piling, flake by
flake in grief. Some sadness, like a child's

cry or a whimpering cub, pulls him back. What presence
inhabits this gash of rock gorge? Carson believes in
horses, mountain lions, in keeping his word, he promises
General Carleton: *All that is connected with*

this canyon will cease to be a mystery. He has orders to
kill Diné who refuse to be saved. Months of pursuit
brought him to this snow-whipped doorway facing
peach orchards hushing the canyon floor, their snow-laced

branches raised heavenward. Loyal as a dog, Carson
flings orders against destiny's door: *starve or submit.* All
summer he burned their cornfields, left livestock carcasses
rotting in pastures. A stink followed him here. His men can

wait until these cold stones give up ghosts or angels. Did Carson
see what he had done when sixty starving Navajos stumbled
down, gaunt acrobats with trembling hands? The skeletal Diné
surrender. The mercy of peach trees surrounds them.

II

Carson's commission ends there in a shudder of light knifing
open the grey snow where Diné wait, last desert riders too
weak to carry frostbitten comrades on the Long March to
Bosque Redondo, the "merciful" reservation experiment of

General Carleton. A procession of Navajos follows pony
soldiers, buckboards carrying grandmothers, the sick who slip
off to the spirit world in the hearse wagons rocking them away
from the land of their ancestors. Diné trudge a path that

America will leave to overgrowth: buckeye trees, blue-silver
salt brush that endures poker-hot sun. What prison
has flowers, fruits, prisoners who will not beg, whose
shamans carry burnt coals incendiary as a prophecy? Spare

them the plans of white men: Carleton to redeem children from
the sin of wildness; Carson, lovable Indian fighter, orders
blankets, mutton for the first frail prisoners of war that walk
the canyon floor past doomed orchards. Then Carson

points upward to two hundred shivering holdouts,
unstraps his axe, and cuts the throat of the first of three
thousand peach trees that fed the Diné. Reports of axe cracks
echo up like cries. Kit Carson, literate in indigenous culture,

has kept his vow.

Mary Carleton, 1864

When Sister Catherine washes
the child's back, her eyes fill. Flakes of
mother's, her sister's blood? Orphaned at
Canyon de Chelly? the Long March?

General Carleton will not say. He stands
in the parlor, resplendent in blue uniform,
gold epaulets, crimson sash, boots polished to
bright black mirrors. He wants to save

this first orphan, a tamable cub, unlike her
relatives who *must be whipped and fear us.*
Navajos are trustworthy as wolves. This is not
Carleton's war but God's, who can use any

instrument, even papist ladies, for His salvific
purpose: to civilize, baptize. Sister Catherine knows
submission too, a relinquishment of will, to be
chosen. She winces, now, as if she, too,

was kicked. The child's uncles, nine hundred of her
ravaged people, are marched even now toward Ft. Sumner.
An exodus, Carleton says, that is *a touching sight . . .*
a whole people found it was their destiny to give

way to the insatiable progress of our race.
Sister Catherine has never questioned authority,
surely not great men, Bishop Lamy, or this
crisp Yankee General who saves innocents.

Catherine dresses the child in blue gingham,
laces high-tops. The grieving orphan stares
at her feet, mice trapped in leather boxes,
slaps them in dust, raising tiny parachutes.

Catherine presents her, *clean,* to the Commander
who sees in her a Navajo future that marches toward
civility, commerce, redemption, even as elderly Diné
walk to death, grateful to leave for another world.

When the Sisters name the child *Mary Carleton*
after her benefactor, Catherine obeys,
gazing into her black eyes for something she cannot
name. When Mary does finally speak,

not Diné language, but "her" American name,
Catherine points to her heart and the child's,
signs the English words General Carleton has never
learned: *Forgive us.*

Beggars: Sisters of Charity

I. Denver, Colorado

The small hand—that twisted a tourniquet
on miners, dressed wounds of gored cowboys,
pulled babies into brass light, soothed the dying
on the threshold of spaciousness—trembles as she writes.

What Catherine remembers has voice as if ink could
sob or laugh the way ecstatic youth love wild
chance, the blessing of those years of Nuevo México.
Sister Catherine Mallon squints into a Denver

morning sun, bends to write because irrepressible Sister Blandina
says history is also a vow, even memories of women who
ask nothing, nurses who fed the destitute, washed broken
dreamers who rode the Santa Fe Trail for gold or glory.

> *My Dear Sister Blandina, You asked me to do the impossible, . . .*
> *to put on paper what happened those many years ago. I have*
> *always wished that those trials and tribulations should be known*
> *to God alone. . . . One thing I do wish, my name not be mentioned.*

II. Vows of Fidelity, Kentucky 1865

Catherine hears a choir intone *Veni Sponsa Christi,*
Come Bride of Christ, as she walks through a sea of candles
carrying the gift of herself, pledged to enter flaming doors
without a glance homeward to this beloved place plunged

in roses. Only twenty-two, Catherine throws her life down,
a shy player who bets everything to be a healer, never regrets
this branding day of vows. She leaves Chapel weeping for
joy, pure desolation. Her companions gather where vases

of pink peonies sit on dark refectory tables as if to say *Rejoice!*
You begin your sacred promise by ending all of this stern, ordinary love.
Chapel bells toll as the sisters lift four valises into a carriage. When
Catherine returns, these ruddy faces will be worn leather pouches.

It seemed as if the hearts of those who were going
and those left behind were torn apart
I can never describe the anguish of that day;
a foreshadowing of . . . crosses

III. Omaha, Nebraska

Four Sisters of Charity, Pauline, Theodosia, Vincent, and Catherine,
board the stagecoach, a quartet of robes, starch, beads. A passenger,
holding an infant, moves toward them, foolish women like herself.
Retired General Wilson stares ahead, annoyed at their need. He touches

his boot, gun holster, reassured, pulls a hat brim over his eyes. On the trail,
Catherine watches sepia cliffs darken as night bleeds lavender. They ride
starlit paths to avoid war parties. When dawn lifts the grey veil, she sees
charred frames of homesteads. Alarmed, General Wilson un-holsters

his pistol, shouts to the driver: *Kiowas!* The pioneer cabins are black crusts
of logs. Kiowa watched once living things—oak, alder, maple—nailed up
boxes, no longer squanderers of seed and shade, lungs of the forest,
asphyxiated by fence-builders. Death then, for death. The iron horse, too,

has trampled grassland where living things breathe. Those who cut
down wildness, its dark luminous body, are enemies.
Catherine writes: *Yes, we were afraid of those poor savages . . .*
but I think the men were more afraid.

IV. Bent's Fort—Deserted

An antiphon of howls echo as their coach rocks
into canyons swabbed in moonlight. Catherine's hunger
makes her hands shake when she reaches to hold the baby.
Not one biscuit for the mother. At the Fort: a hope of sleep, food.

Roof beams of the windowless room sway like a donkey's back.
Catherine turns from its dank smell, filthy cot, a crack where
light seeps. Hollow-eyed and weak, *Sister Vincent threw herself*
on the bed and was asleep with an army of bugs crawling

over her face. The others walk the ghost fort opening rotted doors
to wind-rocked rooms in search of a can of beans. Gold butterflies
flutter in blue silences. Mother's frail hand opens a canteen door pouring
pails of milky light into a spidered room, the shelves stripped.

V. Santa Fe at Last

Four nuns arrive in front of the Bishop's residence, a troupe
of medieval performers, stood up. Lamy, who called for nun nurses,
is traveling. Juana López hurries to *Mother Magdalen: Madre, las Monjas*
llegan! Half-starved, they eat bread, beans, walk Loretto's flower-gashed

garden, sorry to leave for their adobe, dark as midnight. Grit on tables, chairs,
bedclothes. The Sisters of Charity who minister to orphans, the sick, have
    nothing.
They survive, like beggars, on the Lorettos' milk and butter. Catherine's hunger
is for fandango music, the Mexicans who, too, lack milk and butter.

> *Was their hunger arrogance or humility? Did the generosity of the penniless*
> *teach them what America had not? Poor Mexicans see their need, leave*
> *baskets at their door. They ask for curandera Catherine who uses*
> *herbs for sick babies. Las hermanas who take in beggars.*

He was their first beggar and best teacher. Civil War vet, legless, muscled arms
    dragging
his torso into taverns. *He was homeless and friendless, had it not been for the*
    charity of those
poor people, he would probably have died of want, Catherine writes. He lived
    with them for nine
years. His asking *what can I do for you?—Be with us,* they said.

VI. Mining Camps and the Santa Fe Railroad

The Santa Fe Trail belongs to barons who hire immigrants
to hammer silver tracks over hoof and paw paths and to smash
through butte, rim rock to make way for the iron horse snorting
blue smoke into the last silence of the Great Plains.

The rail riders are salesmen, land speculators,
gold seekers, penniless dreamers who spin joyful circles
in Santa Fe's sun-drenched Plaza, then ride to camps
where they are swallowed by mine pits, spit out

in a few years half blind, tubercular, drunks at thirty. These are
Catherine's benefactors. With Sister Pauline she rides
a buck wagon to the Black Range, where four hundred
worm-lunged miners, eyes blind mirrors flecked with

candlelight, dig tunnels eight or ten hours daily. Camps stink
of mule sweat, leather, horse manure, whiffs of sage off
the sand. *Poor fellows*, Catherine says riding days through canyons
rimmed with eyes: mountain lions, coyotes, Kiowa.

VII. The Black Range

Was Catherine naive, delusionally convinced angels rode along,
divine passengers, bumping through arroyos, protectors who pulled
their horses across the raging Gila River, kept the reins taut on
high banks? At the Range, Catherine pities the Scotch Presbyterian

miners who spit bloody phlegm, faces sooted, grizzled, their
small hopes flickering. The men ignore the strange papist supplicants
who offer nothing but entreaties that fly like canaries into
a void. The bosses, who cut open the range with the same tool

that slit men's dreams, shrug off the nuns, who are a nuisance until
measles run the camp felling workers like a logger hacking pine.
The contractors pile their diggers into wagons bound for the nun's
makeshift Santa Fe hospital. Catherine's *poor fellows*

> *came crowding in, and, as we were very poor,*
> *and could not afford beds for all, we gave up our own,*
> *slept on the floor. Those poor men so sick as to be*
> *unable to tell us their names . . .*

VIII. Letters to the Motherhouse

When Catherine and Pauline return to the camps, rose-blotched miners
lift and whirl them. Their burly, sweat-stained hugs exuberant, chaste.
I was their nurse and never referred to their manners of treating us,
but showed them such kindness. . . . They wept like children.

Catherine writes the Motherhouse describing flowers' medicinal power:
how Navajo teachers boil Mormon tea stems for kidney; mesquite leaves
for diarrhea; powder of blue juniper for pain, nausea; jojoba seeds for
childbirth. Every detail except how they raise funds, or the journeys

to the Black Range, their jolt wagon smashed on river rocks, or how
trying to write contributors' names the pencil would fall out of my hand,
they were so cold and numb. My shoes were very much worn . . . a fellow
I had nursed gave me $5 and said, "Now Sister, get yourself warm shoes."

No, none of that in the cheery letters. Only miraculous jimsonweed
for malignant tumors; gourd pulp for skin ulcers. No complaint
of the need for staff, her exhaustion covering wards nightly, arthritic
hip throbbing from the pain of standing eighteen hours.

I was on duty from 5 in the morning to 12 at night and very often I did not eat.
Catherine did report her pleurisy but not that she returned to the Black Range
weak, faint, her deft hands fluttering, a wild goose taken down. The men
place her in a buckboard, whip horses for sixty-five miles. *I was nearly dead.*

No, those stories came years later, long after the Santa Fe Trail ended.
Long after St. Vincent's Hospital reached two floors high with a gleaming
operating room, gowned doctors. Long after the camps were covered
in sand and rabbit prints. Long after she writes of miners who died

in her arms, cowboys nursed through typhoid, Mexicans who paid
with beans and corn. Long after nights in snowbound canyons
which she never revealed until now because *some will read this account
and say 'The sisters must have been mad to expose themselves thus.'*

Not at all. Not at all.

Sister Catherine Mallon

I was twenty-two years old when I took
the gold ring, a moth to Flame.
In sickness or health I burned.

In my beloved New Mexico I was a timid
nurse until I met *los disponibles*.
Bodies shivering, moaning, they begged

us for life, its misery and glory, even
a few days more. I matched a *curandera's*
wisdom to the bravery of the sick.

I carried *los boultos*, bundles of herbs,
medicines . . . what shamans and the desert
placed in my hands, more precious

than nuggets dug from earth's
black heart. Miners prayed for light
even as cold snuffed their candles.

I was given power that vow day in Cincinnati
when I lost the girl I was as if she wandered into
the prairie, a sheep dog who surprised everyone.

Never came back.

Vede Mio Cuore (Look at My Heart) 1850–1894

I. Ligourian Hills Above Genoa, Italy

Giovanna Segale bundles her newborn in a lace
baptismal wrap, climbs Mont' Allegro to La Madre's
altar waiting near stars and balsam. Giovanna offers
the mother of God each of her children. This one,

Rosa Maria, is for the world, this one who will leave
her. Giovanna whispers as if her gift embarrasses.
Here Madre, is my child *to comfort the sorrowful,*
to harbor the harborless, to visit the sick.

II. Cincinnati, Ohio

Tiny Rosa Maria Segale's gaze is heavenward,
not toward God or stars although the habit has shaped
her sense of the possible. It's because she's short, her
students will tower above her, call her *la jefetita*, the little

boss. At sixteen she leaves childhood for the Sisters of Charity.
Fearless as a Marine. Rosa seeks the bold Sisters who enter
Cincinnati's slums as if the drunks and abandoned, prostitutes
hiding wounds of early crucifixions, were family. Before

she will be named Sister Blandina, teenage Rosa Maria
stands in the Motherhouse entrance. Small as a fifth grader,
she looks up to Mother Superior's eyes and does not blink.
Ciao, she says to her brother, sisters. *Grazi, Mama, grazi.*

A blue September sky floats opals of light through elms
inking a grotto where Rosa Maria writes her older sister Maddalena,
who has turned down her third and last suitor. Pity Cincinnati boys
in the garden of virgins who give grapes and bread to the poor.

III. Trinidad, Colorado, 1872

The twenty-two-year-old Sister Blandina is bound for crimson
skies, blue mesas, a dirt town where natives, *desperados*, and missionaries
bleed for the world anonymously. Bullies and the meek
beneath a brutal sun, a night of stars that cannot calm the newcomers

who want what the land will refuse, immovable as heaven. Blandina
wants God, and, not incidentally, outcasts. Both inseparable to her.
Her theology is a gambler's: *never turn away from hardship*
and miracles show up . . . if not, bluff until the fourth ace is dealt.

First hardship in Trinidad, Colorado: no school, no church.
Blandina's letter to her sister Maddelena, now named Sister Justina,
is a gospel of vinegar and honey: *My dearest . . . it may please you
to know my attitude. Vede mio cuore (Look at my heart).*

*I wish I had many hands and feet, a world full of hearts . . .
so much one sees to be done, and so few to do it.
I have adopted this plan: Do whatever presents itself,
and never omit anything because of hardship or repugnance.*

To build Trinidad's Public School Number One with no money
Blandina has a plan: *Borrow a crowbar, get on the roof, and detach adobes.
"What are you doing, Sister?" and I will answer, "Tumbling down
this structure to rebuild it before fall term."* Their wives send them:

carpenters who shout up to the tiny figure wedging a crowbar,
merchants who bring lime, sandstone, brushes for whitewash,
mould carriers who tote mortar under supervision of a black-bonneted
commander who hikes her skirts to carry buckets in the line. Her friend

Rafael, Chief of the Utes, trusts one white, *Hermana*—she who knows
his language, not Ute but wordless sorrow. He asks Blandina to bury
his son. *Oh Justina,* she writes, *generations to come will blush for these deeds.
Rafael said, "Shall I throw him away like a dog? . . . white men call us dogs!"*

IV. Billy and Blandina, Colorado

Blandina is umping a baseball game when Billy the Kid's
sidekick jingles his stallion into the school yard. *Hombre* is theater:
tips his gold-stitched sombrero as his horse bows. Outlaw wears
red velvet toreador britches, green waist coat, the saddle cloth is

gold. No one snickers. It is his last performance before a shotgun blast.
Toreador is bleeding to death because Trinidad physicians refuse
to cut the bullet out of his thigh. Nurse Blandina feeds him for weeks,
a rabbit with a mangled leg thrown in an abandoned hut. His pal

Billy keeps score: doctors, soon-to-be-dead men; Blandina, angel ally.
The Kid loves spunk. Blandina demands payback: *spare town doctors.*
Sister Justina winces at the letter's bravura. Billy doesn't. *Dear Justina,*
Billy said, 'Sister, any time my pals and I can serve you, you will find us ready.'

The town docs who stitch bleeders never knew they were flung like angels
through the breath of wind that Billy and Blandina opened like a window.
What of the human heart (Justina)? . . . One moment diabolical, the next angelical.
If you ever get this journal you will see how little fear I have of Billy's gang.

V. Billy's Gang Surrounds the Stagecoach

The driver is ashen, passengers stuff coins in boots,
unstrap revolvers. Blandina tells them *put up your guns,*
leans into whipping grit so that Billy sees the bonnet.
Bandit gallops forward until he sees her:

> *our eyes met; he raised his large brimmed hat*
> *with a wave and bow . . . then stopped to give his wonderful antics*
> *on bronco maneuvers . . . Sister Augustine cannot understand*
> *why I had no fears of Billy the Kid's gang.*

VI. Near McCarthy's Grading Camp

Apaches! Halt. Armed townsmen stop the nun's wagon.
On a high ridge Apaches in war paint surround the town shooters,
demand the murderer who shot dead a starving Apache
who "stole" discarded camp food. Blandina's letter to Justina

lays out her plan: *bracing myself with prayer . . .*
I slowly walked up to meet them. Apaches, too, had a plan:
They must give us the murderer, Nana! Sister Blandina, Nana, gets
this justice, tells the citizen army to turn the murderer over.

> *The advice is given . . . as my conscience dictates.*
> *I'm not certain that theology bears me out. . . .*
> *When you come to Albuquerque*
> *Please, Justina, don't mention this incident to me.*

VII. Jornada del Muerto

The open jolt wagon rocks two shivering nuns into a heavy snow
drooping their cotton caps. Lost on the *Dead Man's Road*
Blandina drapes blankets over Sister Catherine Mallon still
whooping from pneumonia, then she covers the driver's frostbitten

ears, hums a hymn, tells the driver to *Give reins, mules will find
the road.* Mule angels carry them across powder to Hopi land where children
starve because agents stole food. Blandina, rarely powerless, reaches
for her beads, fingers raw and red. Feebly promises to tell the President.

VIII. Back to Trinidad After Twelve Years in New Mexico

Pupils from Public School Number One line a mud road
calling *Hermana, Hermana*, a burst of applause,
ruddy farmers, cowboys, mothers who remember
beloved *Jefetita*, first teacher, first to believe in them. One

hand in the crowd points to St. Rafael Hospital.
It is a beggar's hand, it's *comadre* Catherine Mallon,
who took whiskey money from ruined miners. Old friend
nods proudly at the hospital as if the angels who carried them

out of a frozen desert had planned this—a surgical theater,
porcelain tables, white sheets for those who have no angels,
no blankets, bread, no one with whom to risk everything, no
Sisters of Charity *comadre* on the broken trails.

IX. Adios, Trinidad

Like a fox cub rejected by his mother, Blandina's old student
trusts no one, not even the nun who saved him from prison.
He leads a politician's group who press the school board
to oust the papists. Sisters must defrock or quit teaching.

Trinidad is tamed: outlaws and nuns forbidden.
*So this is the end of twenty-two years in Public School Number One
opened when Trinidad was governed by the best shot-gun . . .
(when) Sisters used every effort to quell the daily storms . . .*

Adios, Trinidad of heart-pains and consolations! Jefetita rides
the Chili Line east, watches dawn roll off the Sangre de Cristos.
Train clacks past clusters of blue spruce, piñon,
muscles up over butter canyons . . . resolute.

Those Who Ride

Comanche Chief, 1850–1911

I. Palo Duro Canyon

Quanah Parker, Whites with grey eyes like yours,
come with papers, black marks slithering snake-words.
Mother are there no Whites like you? Mother, Nadua,
wait for me when I am done, for we are spiders all.

Your rain-cloud eyes grateful: to wolf and antelope,
night-candles, ocotillo, rain lily and moss rose. Desert
wisdoms unable to save Comanches. Hide your people
behind the waterfalls of chinaberry trees at Palo Duro

Canyon, sanctuary of willow and rock-gorge, safe place
until Yellow Leaves the Moon month when Mackenzie's
soldiers belly-crawl to the canyon lip, aim repeating rifles
at your aunts, cousins, the volleys stampeding panicked horses

pounding through blood and bodies. Mothers cover babies with
their last protection, breath and breast. Screams, ricochets,
wails for the dead, until silence and smoke rise like butterflies
in the ripped air. Warriors cradle dying children, wait for another

world. Some escape Palo Duro's death chamber, carry memory,
a bag of thorns thrown on America's altars. Run Quanah! Fly
through canyon doors sobbing in your freedom, a stench of death
on your buckskin, stains that never wash out. The cries you carry.

II. Surrender, 1875

As Chief, unable to bear another massacre,
your babies flung like gutted rabbits in fields,
you will walk into Ft. Sill. Behind you, ancestors
dance in red dust, your father, Peta Nocona,

wounded by Texas Rangers at the Pease River.
Did Chief Nocona's dying eyes see Rangers
capture your white mother Cynthia Ann Parker,
your sister Topasannah, there, where the river turned

pink? Did Chief Nocona see his orphan Quanah run off
with Kwahadi Comanches, a ten-year-old mixed-blood
who did not cry, a wolf cub running, smoke-eyes
seeing in the dark, crossing a river stained with father's

blood? Did the boy hide in the perfumed desert,
cactus cradling field mice warmer than Quanah whose name
meant "fragrance"? Comanches call him Tseeta,
name him Chief after a raid on buffalo hunters where,

wounded, he still carried the fallen Howeah on his back.
This same Chief surrenders at Ft. Sill. Tseeta, you are
Quanah again. Now you must learn your mother's tongue which
she never spoke to you. You learn the English word property.

III. Jerome Commission, 1892

*Commissioner this land is ours, just like your farm is yours
But for one reason we cannot hold onto ours, because
on the right hand is what you are trying to do,
and on the left hand is the Dawes bill.*

Quanah speaks a fourth language—sign, reads each hand's
betrayal. Senator Dawes explains: *greed was
the element most lacking in Indian societies—without it
they could not hope to reach the white man's level of civilization.*

Quanah Parker kisses his pony, enters the place of fences,
allotments, laws. His mother escaped this prison twice.
After Whites recaptured her and Topasannah,
she bolted with the child pummeling into high grass

begging the prairie for a path to Comanche land.
But mother and child, deft as fox, can't outrun
a mounted posse of rescuers. Returned to civilization
Topasannah cannot breathe inside the coffin house where

they are safe. When she dies, her despairing mother escapes
a second, last time: she kills Cynthia Parker, dies as
Nadua, a Comanche far from home. Her white relatives dress
"Cynthia" in gingham for the burial.

IV. 1911, Oklahoma Res

Forty years later Quanah brings his mother to Polk Oak Indian
Cemetery, his own sleep place. *Mother, Great Eagle calls my name.*
Dying, he is attended by Dr. Knox Beal, but his wives ask Beal kindly
to leave. Their medicine man, Quas-E-I, embraces Tseeta,

who slips from the holy man's arms to rise in Great Eagle's
flight: *Father in heaven this our brother is coming.* These
moccasins on the path to the Mystery of hidden prairies
unstaked, free.

Chiefs: Crook, Cochise, Standing Bear, 1870s –1880s

I. Apache Land

Three hundred and fifty Bluecoats jingle over sand,
twist in their saddles as if they feel dry air crack
open a low whistle of arrows. Ahead, in Chiricahua
mountains, eyes watch a lariat of vultures swing

wide. Horses spook, too, frightened by their rider's
swallowed inhales. Lt. Colonel Crook rides lead.
His soldiers will testify: I obeyed the orders
of my commanding officer.

> *My orders. Apaches call me Grey Wolf. In the new*
> *moon I see shadows move in donkey mountains.*
> *My hair is turning silver, my eyes fallen stars.*
> *Here rabbit tracks are slight as breath, ghost ponies*
> *whinny in canyons. I hear coyote opera yowl across*
> *this dazzled theater of blue flax and gophers.*

Crook bobbles on a mule named Apache. Behind him
five cavalry companies follow the yellow ass.
Miles of flies, rattlers, mountain lions, shadows cross
moon-slashed canyons, a tremble of hooves bites

hard, fast. Cochise, swift speck ahead, vanishes into
twilight, rider crossing a magenta desert darkening. He
outruns Grey Wolf, pounds the soft grey carpet
sewn into a violet horizon, heads for Santa Fe to

find the Star Chief General who outranks Crook. Warrior
seeks an end. He sees what Grey Wolf sees:
trophies of antlers, bleached bones, a desert reliquary.
What dies here belongs to sun and fang. What can he

save? His starving people, their mountains where long light
falls? Ride, Cochise, ask White Painted Woman for Power,
ask the spirit of Chief Mangas—who trusted a Bluecoat
truce flag—to raise his mutilated body and whisper

you home. Let ancestors ride too, an army of the broken,
chanting your pony to speed. Ride, Cochise, ride. Grey Wolf can
only be what he is—wolf. Crook whispers to his mule: *back,
Apache, back*, signals the column's return, pats Apache's sweated neck.

> *This enemy I love flawed by Apache honor.*
> *Cochise cannot lie, his only salvation.*
> *Oh Great Power of primrose, of bluebells, of breath and cry,*
> *burn Apaches brighter, last wild hearts. Forgive our Fathers*
> *who knew what blood would stain these rocks, who unleashed*
> *hunters, miners, cowboys and thieves . . . wolves like me.*

Once Apaches rode inside the great Sonora Silence, their ponies flew
the house of sand and tumbleweed. Now destiny covers the sand with
blue spiders, a wedge advancing. Jackrabbits, gophers, hawk run with
Apaches, doomed, clever, faster than Grey Wolf. For now.

Cochise runs mountain stairs until his hair turns grey as tears. Until Bluecoats
corral Apaches at Ft. Tularosa, place of flies, mud water where he cannot go even
for his people. He reaches for mother's gift, necklace of hummingbird feathers:
how tiny creatures give themselves when it is time to leave the road of sky.

> *The White people have looked for me long. I am here! . . . The world*
> *was not always this way. God made us not as you: we were born*
> *like the animals in the dry grass . . . When I was young I walked all*
> *over this country, east and west, and saw no other people than Apaches.*
> *After many summers I walked again and found another race of people*
> *had come to take it. How is it? Why is it Apaches wait to die?*

II. Chief Standing Bear, Nebraska Winter

General Crook loves Chief Standing Bear, too, the Ponca
chief who carries dying children through blizzards. Ponca women,
children punch moccasins, stiff and bloody, through ice crusts,
stain the prairies where they are force-marched from Nebraska

to Oklahoma. Ponca pallbearers heft snow-piled slings cradling
bodies that no longer shiver. One lone hawk spirals in dull winter
light when Standing Bear's last son falls. The chief stands in a prairie
that holds rabbit and field mice against its ice-caked breast.

When he was dying . . . he begged me
to take him back to our old burying ground
by the Swift Running Water, the Niobrara.
I promised. When he died, I, and those with me,
put his body in a box and then in a wagon
and we started north.

It is Snows Thaws Moon, coldest month when Standing Bear turns
back. He lifts his boy into a wagon pulled by starving horses who
plow toward home. The renegades know their fate. At Fort Omaha,
Crook receives orders from the War Department: arrest

Standing Bear's party, Crook prays: wake me before first light, give me
enemies I deserve. The guardhouse where Standing Bear waits stinks
of manure. When Crook enters, Standing Bear says nothing. Crook turns
from the Chief's grief. After that, Crook was ruined.

> *Standing Bear gave us no absolution, no condemnation. I entered a fouled*
> *cage where he stood erect, defeated. I am a patriot. I am unforgiven.*
> *I still see him turn away. I did petition the Courts for him but the sin was*
> *beyond me.*
> *Who could bear Standing Bear's words?*
> *I, Standing Bear, thought God intended us to live. But I was mistaken.*
> *God intended to give the country to white people, and we are to die.*

III. Crook and Geronimo

Standing Bear unravels Crook, makes an agnostic warrior. As Commander
of Arizona, Crook rails at agents who starve Apaches, scolds settlers *unscrupulous*
white men trying to rouse to violent action so Apaches could be driven from
the reservation, leaving it for land-grabbing. Honor now is a striptease.

He wears no uniform, a pith helmet for a General's cap. Trusts only his mule.
Eyes keener, he sniffs danger in his own pack. More feral, General Crook fears
frontier citizens who steal Apache land, fears his own Great Chief. The President,
who believes what he reads, wants Geronimo hung. Last warrior prances

the Sierras, his stocking-hooved ponies ride roads
no soldier finds. But Crook's Apache scouts track their magician.
At Canyon of Faults, they find the trickster. Geronimo waits
in shadow, owes nothing to a long-toothed wolf or to Apache turncoats.

Warriors and Scouts watch both chiefs as purple snuffs canyon light;
it is the hour of wolf and cougar. Apache scouts do not argue with darkness
opening the first blue star, they tell Geronimo he was never their Chief.
Crook is tired of orders, of Geronimo's cleverness, is weary of the chase.

Crook is a caricature—newspapers report the General who coddles Apaches,
fears Geronimo. Good citizens of the southwest petition for security,
Apache removal. Grey Wolf, exhausted, nudges his donkey forward
into the starlit canyon where he promises Geronimo what he can . . . nothing.

Geronimo promises Grey Wolf to run no more. But he does.
Mountains sigh when he finally surrenders, lonely
for his family who wait for the singing pine, cottonwood,
rose canyons. Geronimo's longing fills Apacheria:

> *I cannot think we are useless or God would not have created us.*
> *We are all the children of one God. . . . The sun, the darkness, the winds*
> *are all listening to what we have to say. . . . I was born on the prairies*
> *where the wind blew free and there was nothing to break the light . . .*

Crook has his sins packed up, carries them everywhere:
> *Silence can trick you. An owl, a wolf's cry can alter perception of distance.*
> *Like clabberless bells, military medals report nothing here: every ribbon*
> *bleeds. My promise of land is as good as any white man's.*

> *General Miles orders Apaches to Florida, a swamp where children*
> *cough, fever. Warriors pitch rocks into circles, drink mescal,*
> *remember the sacred place. Older children don't cry when soldiers*
> *tear them from elders, pull them onto the Iron Horse bound for*

> *Carlisle Indian school in Pennsylvania. Don't cry when their*
> *shorn hair falls like dark animal pelts into piles of leggings, ribboned*
> *blouses, moccasins. All burned. Their ghosts wear starched collars,*
> *ties, suits, high-top shoes. Ghosts' cheekbones are beautiful.*

> *Children are called stoic who refuse this salvation. Stoic, who*
> *brave a cousin's small crucifixion, stoic when they sit in infirmaries*
> *watching their friends die of pleurisy, despair. Fifty in all,*
> *one after another, nailed on the gibbet of civilization.*

Chief Standing Bear

Every vow I kept, kept me. The last
to my dying son was for the famished
road, a Ponca road of the walking

dead. The vow of a father who walked
in the dying footsteps of his daughter, hundreds
too weak to reach the Oklahoma reservation.

A vow against shame which is what fell,
hard as snow, on soldiers who drove
skeletons five hundred miles to pens. My vow,

a river circling rocks, had no beginning,
no end. How useless such a vow before
U.S. law: Indians *were not human*, had

no claims in court. Our ravaged silence ended
when I, who had nothing, rose, extended
my hand, spoke to the judge:

That hand is not the color of yours,
but if I pierce it, I shall feel pain.
If you pierce your hand, you also feel pain.

The blood that will flow will be
the same color as yours. I am a man.
The same God made us both.

My promise, trudged through snowbanks,
ice and howl, exceeded vindication,
a Judge's honor, or the imagination

of conquerors. My raised hand, raw with frostbite
from pulling ponies through cracked rivers, a betrayed
hand that dug my children's graves.

General Crook

A soldier's promise is a debt
ordered by the venerated who
wear colored ribbons and silver

medals. They want attention, salutes,
want an acolyte to genuflect before
the Commander in Washington

until my knees grew weak
and the blue-coated jefes
pinned on my stars, having torn

them from the bleeding sky.
I, who have brought them blood
and bonnet, enter a warrior's paradise

shimmering with honors
in spite of my oddball tactics
unacceptable in lesser gods:

how I rode mules, seduced Apache guides
for America's destiny. Until the cost of it
was called in, that time with Standing Bear.

Now I am a general who rides with ghosts
and martyrs as if heaven were not somewhere
else but here, a paradise strewn with dead buffalo.

I no longer salute, which is blasphemous.
My discipline is dead, shot like a wounded pony.
My medals lie rusted. I seek absolution from

prisoners I've made. Savages who opened my
heart: Geronimo who tricked it, Cochise who named it,
Standing Bear who broke it.

Geronimo

Words, you Whites, want words.
Nothing, I give you nothing.
Here, stones, the Sierra Madres has

something you can't use:
the witness of rocks who speak
the language of mountains. We are

this land, stones inside the rain, inside
the mountain which keeps the graves.
Here, Grey Wolf, is another lie, hard

as granite, I give it to you, call it sustenance.
Eat—Why do I give you promise after promise,
rock instead of bread? I want to break your

trust the way Mexicans broke my wife, my mother,
my three babies, their scalps in blood rivers. What
fear can you offer to a dead man? After that

I did not pray . . . I had no purpose left. I could not
call back my loved ones. I could not bring back
dead Apaches but I could rejoice in . . . revenge.

So no, I'm not trustworthy. I am wily,
a coyote slipping into shadow. Is it
honor to promise open land and pen us

at San Carlos, that stink hole? See our
lonely ponies, our mountains pouring.
What did you expect . . . truth? Whose?

Every vow a snakebite; every safe place
a trap. Treachery? Oh, I am a holy trickster,
son of White Painted Woman. I love mescal,

which is all I have left of escape, a poison as greedy
as the givers. Mescal . . . there is something of use.
We are not.

Prophecy, 1840–1887

I. Ojo Caliente , Apacheria, 1840

Masked Chihenne Apaches carry flaming ocotillo
branches that float a wreath of light on canyon floors
where they dance in the breach, chests painted with suns
as if the heart were bright as buttercups. They step, step,

sing to the hours, gold hearts humming to the sixteen-year-old
about to become a woman. Lozen, sponged in oil and water
by naaikish, her godmother, stands in beaded buckskin,
ready for her ceremony. When she dances, the men's hissing

cadence of deer-hoof rattles remind Useen, Giver of Life,
that a daughter is asking for Power, asking White Painted Woman
for wisdom. So it is that a girl of solitude becomes a shaman.
In the cave of her loneliness, vision comes.

II. The Bluecoats, 1848

Lozen can sense enemy presence, a flutter of the pulse like a small
bird's warning. She who trusts Spirit risks invisibility and power,
whispers her stallion into Bluecoat's corral, stampedes sixty-eight
horses whose shadow hooves hammer the open range, a wild river

moving the darkness. Had the ponies waited for her to enter stillness
which belonged to them? She who sees does not ride with women but
warrior chiefs: Nana, her brother Victorio, Geronimo. How does she
coax horses from cavalry camps, wheeling them toward mountain's

secret doors? Lozen, thief and prophet, sits at council but dares not
speak. It is the way of her Power, to seek nothing. When women's
horses panic at churlish Rio Bravo, she leads her mount into whitewater,
plunges back for grandfather's pony sweeping down stream. Fearless,

she believes Ussen loves Apaches enough to outsmart
pale-eyes whose mules eat more than her people. When Chihenne
are trapped like hobbled ponies at San Carlos Res, she tells
Victorio that Ussen asks too much. Beloved brother—

who took rear guard, the most dangerous, Chief who sued
for peace, who begs White Eyes for their own land, who finally
stops begging, who no Apache scout can find—Victorio tells
Lozen that the Giver of Life runs with the people,

starves too, weeps when they fall, loves Lozen, chosen one.
But Victorio, named for victory, no longer believes. He sends Lozen
to midwife Eclode's labor in the safety of Mescalero Res.
Victorio, perfect shot, who can walk up a cliff drop, who knows

Bluecoats are too many, knows Mexicans are closing in, knows
Lozen will lead the Chihenne to San Carlos if he falls, knows how
many will die of malaria there, knows the next bullet is his.
When eagle screams, Lozen races her pony toward a sky bitter as wine.

III. Chief Victorio is Killed, 1880

She drinks stained twilight, pouring over cactus, jackrabbits, juniper,
desert witnesses already lonely. After Victorio's death Geronimo
seeks her prophecy. Lozen dare not share her visions:
all fangs, blood. When the Grey Wolf takes Geronimo's surrender,

Lozen walks women and children to San Carlos, their dogs trot
into the desert to die, a circle of black wings float high.
After Grey Wolf leaves for Nebraska, the snake, General Miles,
orders last warriors of the desert to Florida where Lozen unpacks

her final medicine, not prophecy, she can't bear the future. She tells
the children White Painted Woman is singing for them, dancing near
the trees of heaven, daring them to Spirit even as their warriors drink
corn whiskey and puke. *Vision will not desert you,* she says. *Remember,*

remember. Even as the children shipped to Carlisle weaken, they sing
to Useen, weep in infirmaries, hold hands when the coffins arrive. Even then
they chant Apache prayers and *remember.* Removed to a barracks
in Alabama, Lozen sucks drenched air into lungs collapsed by TB.

Does she welcome release, whisper Useen in a final, strangled
voice? Does she see Ojo Caliente, wind shaking cottonwood
leaves, Apache horses gamboling beneath pearl skies? Remember,
she told the children, *the land has heart, remembers you.*

Those Who Ride

A sacred voice is calling
        —Black Elk

Those who ride, ride in sorrow.
Blandina watches mesas burn bright
as sunflowers, scolds her useless hands

open on her lap like broken wings. Juniper
blurs by hour after hour. At desert's end,
the hooded choir of *los piñones* bows silent.

General Crook rides across bones.
Each stone a solitary witness,
a rain of memories drenching.

The General only knows military orders
without which the trail can devour
him, ruthless as a hungry wolf.

A grey wolf he could never recognize,
the soldier he was before he was a man
that time when he did not love the wolf.

Who follows him now, howling
circling. Is it his own shadow?
Is it memory with its starving need?

Who boards trains, boards in grief.
Apaches rolling toward Florida swamps.
Geronimo watching the ghosts who

sing to the people but cannot comfort
them penned into cars, a heavy humid
scent seeping in of land without mountains.

Apache children are herded
onto trains bound east to cold mountains
and a curriculum for dying.

The Millennium

The nuns have left small footprints in
a desert that expects no allies. Wind and sand
cover the histories of saints and sinners.

But the people are partisans, carry altars,
candles. Padre Martínez's memoria burns on.
The gringos still look for Billy the Kid's grave.

Apaches and Navajos watch canyons' ochre
silence, forgive the wild horses who run
across the blood floors of ancestors,

forgive those ghosts who walked Carleton's
frozen road, their grandparents' terrible courage,
forgive the Spirit. Forget nothing.

The Loretto and Charity sisters accompany
the wretched as if they held Mystery
in torn, filthy breast pockets. What do they cling

to as their time ends, the hour of nuns
archaic as cowboys? Their novitiates empty,
grand motherhouse rattling with white-haired

sisters who sign away the green lawns, barns,
refectories, convents . . . and rejoice. Diminished,
barely able to care for the elderly, they

give away the store without regret.
Who taught them these wild ways?

Acknowledgments

Parts of this book were first published as follows:

"Geronimo," *New Mexican Poetry Review*, V01.1, N0.1, 2009
"General Crook," *New Mexican Poetry Review*, V01.1, N0.1, 2009
"Manifest Destiny," *El Malpais Review*, V01.1, N0.1, 2010
"Nuevo México," *El Malpais Review,* V01.1, N0.1, 2010

I would like to thank: Judith Kitchen for astute editing advice; Allen Schwartz for encouragement; poet Tony Mares for generously promoting a gringa's read on his New Mexican history; UNM Press poetry editor Barrett Price for his kindness and belief in this narrative; and UNM Press Director Luther Wilson for his availability and affability.

Special thanks to UNM Press editors Beth Hadas and Elise McHugh for shepherding this book. To Mary Ann Corley, who supported this, read it over many times, and made critical suggestions. More than anyone, she helped make this book possible.

In gratitude to Meinrad Craighead whose painting "Moons of the Vernal Equinox, 1987" from *Meinrad Craighead: Crow Mother and Dog God, A Retrospective*, (Petaluma, CA: Pomegranate Communications), 2003, is the book's cover image. New Mexican and mystical, Meinrad's work stuns, challenges, and inspires. I am deeply honored to have her painting on this book's cover.

¡Gracias a todos!

Sources

I've used the following sources in framing these poems. Although the historical figures' narrations are imagined, I have also used direct quotes from the actual recorded speech or diary of the person speaking.

Introduction

Quote from Rina Swentzell and Phillip Cassadore, "Honoring Our Elders," www.comanchelodge.com/quotes.

"Los Ladrones (The Thieves)" and "Bishop Lamy"

Pay Ray John de Aragon, *Padre Martinez and Bishop Lamy* (Santa Fe: Sunstone Press), 2006.

Paul Horgan, *Lamy of Santa Fe* (New York: Farrar, Straus & Giroux), 1975.

E. A. Mares et al., *Padre Martinez: New Perspectives From Taos* (Taos: Millicent Rogers Museum), 1988.

"Las Hermanas de la Luz (Sisters of Light)"

Patricia Jean Manion SL, *Beyond the Adobe Wall: The Sisters of Loretto in New Mexico, 1852–1894* (Independence, MO: Two Trails Publishing), 2001.

Mary Jean Straw Cook, *Loretto: The Sisters and Their Santa Fe Chapel* (Santa Fe: Museum of New Mexico Press), 2002.

"Sister Catherine Mallon"

"Sister Catherine Mallon's Journal," Pt. 1 and 2, ed. Thomas Richter, *New Mexico Historical Review* 52 (Spring and Summer), 1977.

"Vede Mi Cuore (Look at My Heart), 1850–1894"

Sister Blandina Segale, *At the End of the Santa Fe Trail* (Milwaukee: Bruce Publishing Co.), 1945.

"Canyon de Chelly, 1864"

Hampton Sides, *Blood and Thunder* (New York: Doubleday), 2006, pp. 346–68.

Dee Brown, *Bury My Heart at Wounded Knee* (New York: Holt, Rinehart and Winston), 1981, pp. 22–33.

"Chiefs: Crook, Cochise, Standing Bear, 1870s–1880s"

Dee Brown, *Bury My Heart at Wounded Knee* (New York: Holt, Rinehart and Winston), 1981, pps. 200–211, 341–44.

Dan L. Thrapp, *The Conquest of Apacheria* (Norman: University of Oklahoma Press), 1967.

Helen Hunt Jackson, *A Century of Dishonor* (New York: Harper & Brothers), 1881.

"Chief Standing Bear"

David J. Wishart, *An Unspeakable Sadness* (Lincoln: University of Nebraska Press), 1995, pp. 132–45.

Dave Harm, "Standing Bear: A Missed Opportunity," www.Authorsden.com, June 23, 2005.

"Geronimo"

Odie Faulk, *The Geronimo Campaign* (New York: Oxford University Press), 1969.

Dee Brown, *Bury My Heart at Wounded Knee*, (New York: Holt, Rinehart and Winston), 1981, pp. 372–86.

Stephen Melville Barrett and Frederick Turner, introduction to *Geronimo: His Own Story: The Autobiography of a Great Patriot Warrior* (New York: Dutton), 1970.

"Prophecy, 1840–1887"

Peter Aleshire, Lozen: *Woman Warrior* (New York: St. Martin's Press), 2001.

Kimberly Buchanan, *Apache Women Warriors* (Austin: University of Texas Press), 1986.

Zimmerman Library Center for Southwest Research at the University of New Mexico.